SALLY NOLL
OFF AND COUNTING

Greenwillow Books, New York

FOR KATE

Publisher, Greenwillow Books,
a division of William
Morrow & Company, Inc.,
105 Madison Avenue,
New York, N.Y. 10016.
Printed in the
United States of America
First Edition

10 9 8 7 6 5 4 3 2

Library of Congress Cataloging in Publication Data
Noll, Sally.   Off and counting.
Summary: Presents the numbers one through ten as a
wind-up frog hops along bumping into various groups
of toys including three toy trains, four hobby horses,
and ten soldiers.   [1. Stories in rhyme.
2. Toys—Fiction.   3. Counting]
I. Title.
PZ8.3.N736Of 1984   [E]   83-16366
ISBN 0-688-02795-4
ISBN 0-688-02796-2 (lib. bdg.)

Windup Frog lives in a shop
and likes to count from hop to hop.
Starting out with number one,
he counts the toys until he's done.

Up, up he climbs ... steady and mounting. Away he goes, off and counting ...

one one one one

1

one one one one

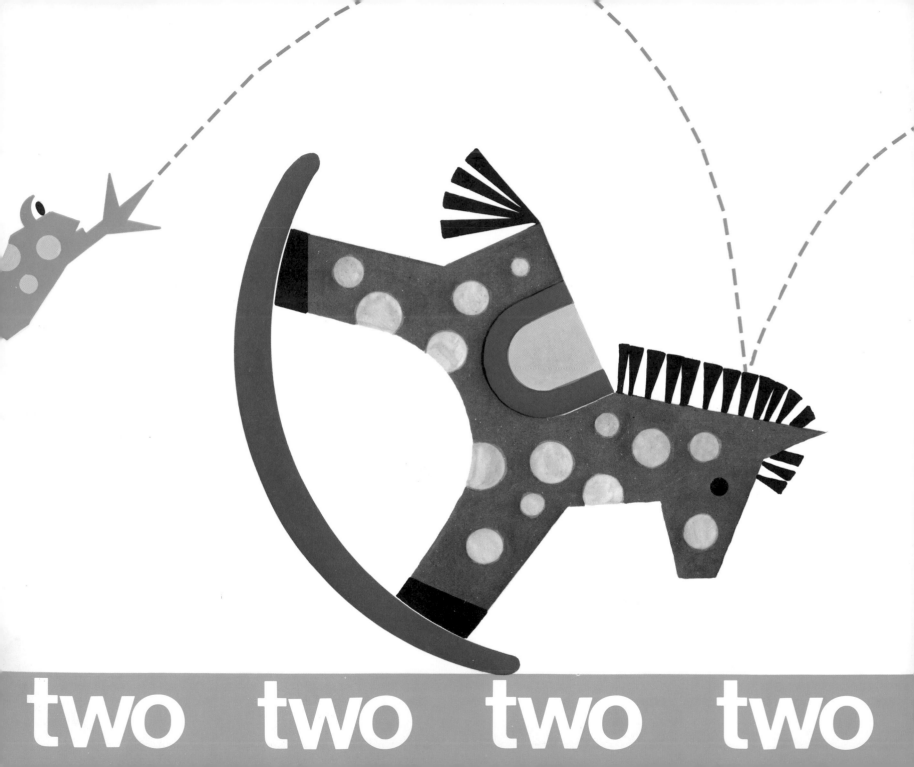

two two two two

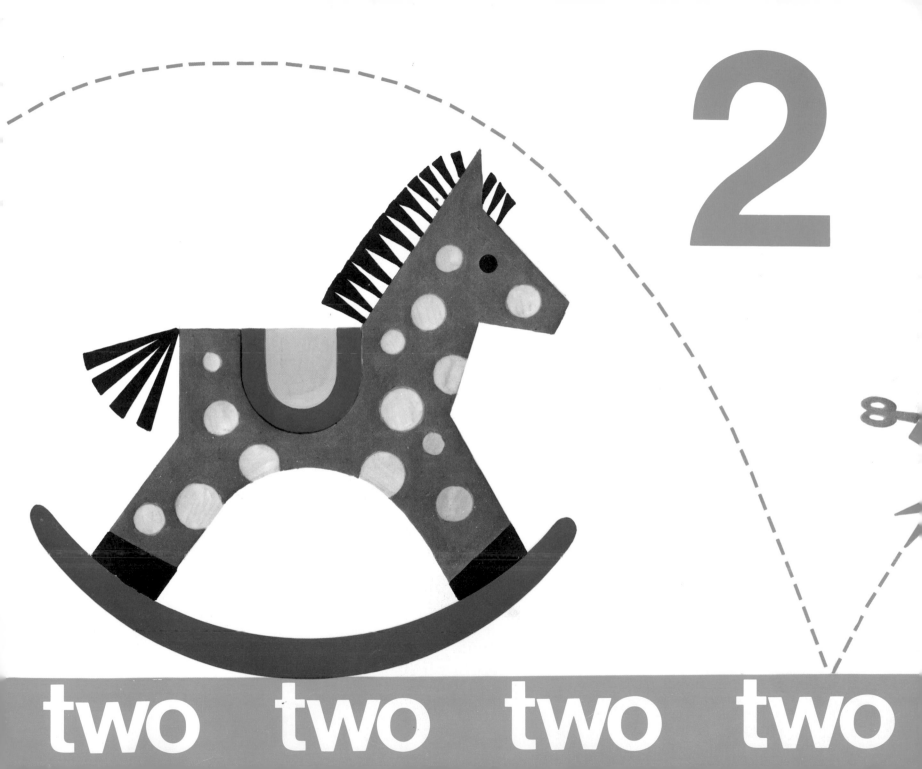

2

two two two two

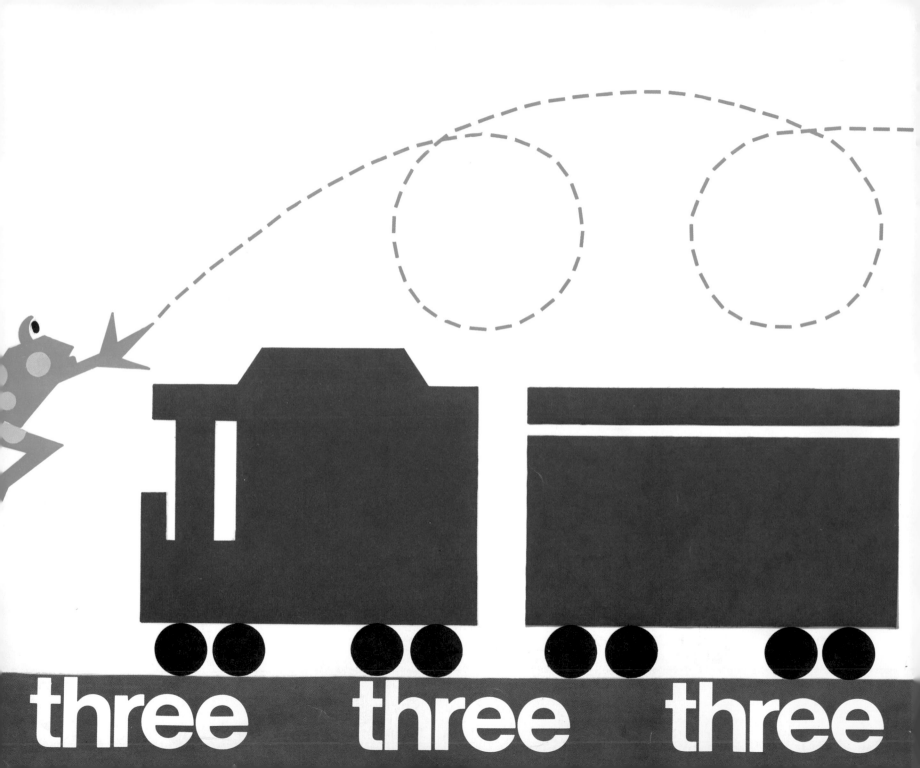

three three three

3

three three three

four four four four

4

four four four four

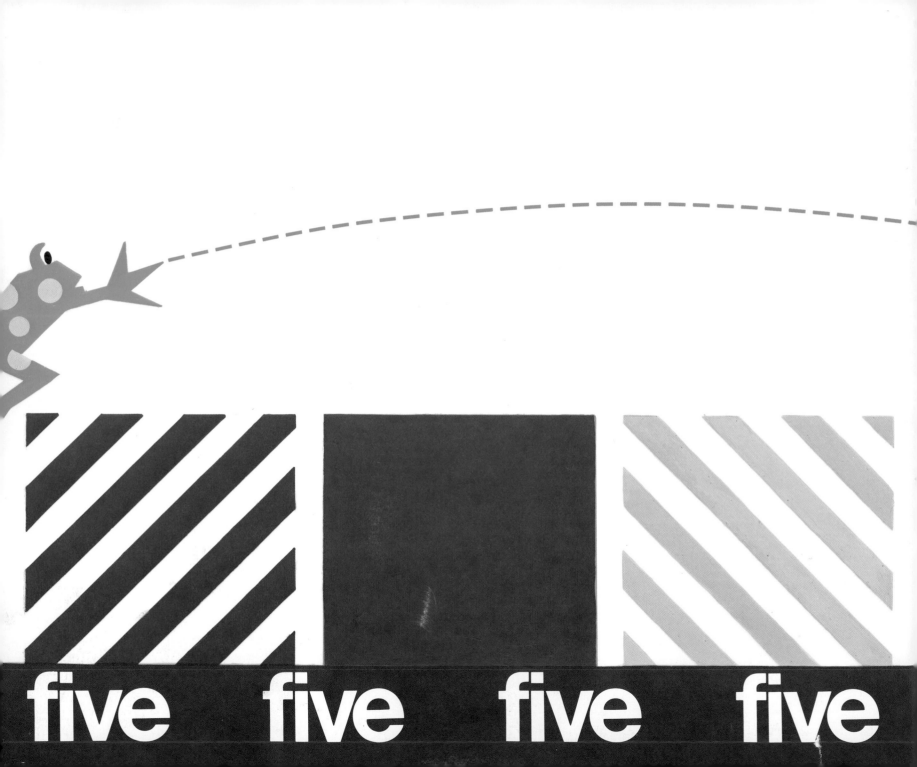

five   five   five   five

5

five   five   five   five

six six six six six

6

six six six six six

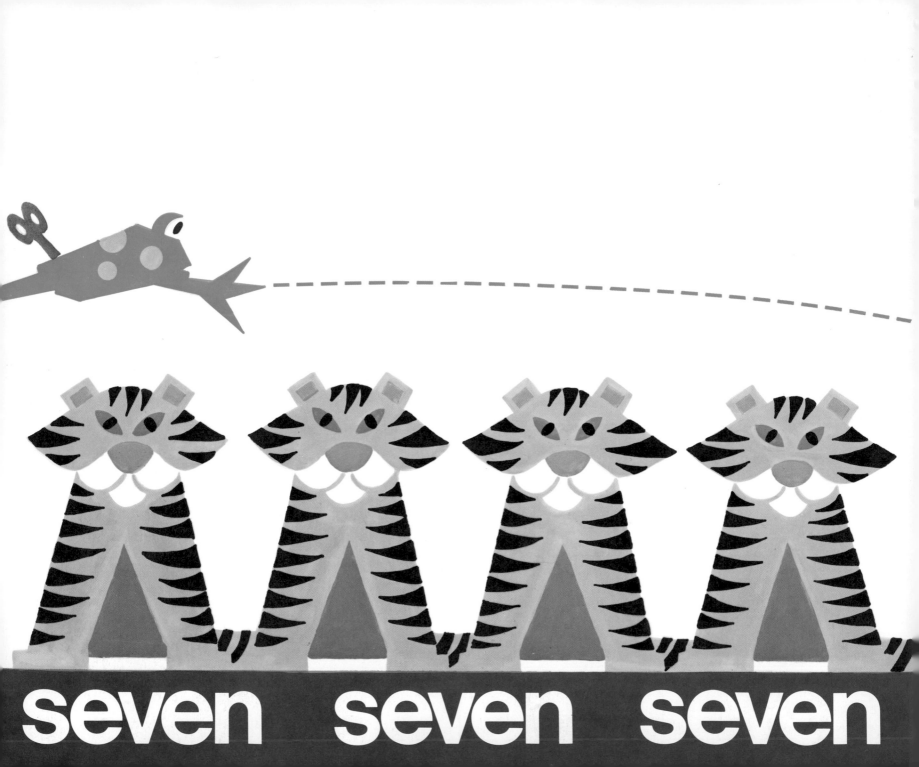

seven seven seven

7

seven seven seven

eight eight eight

eight eight eight

nine nine nine nine

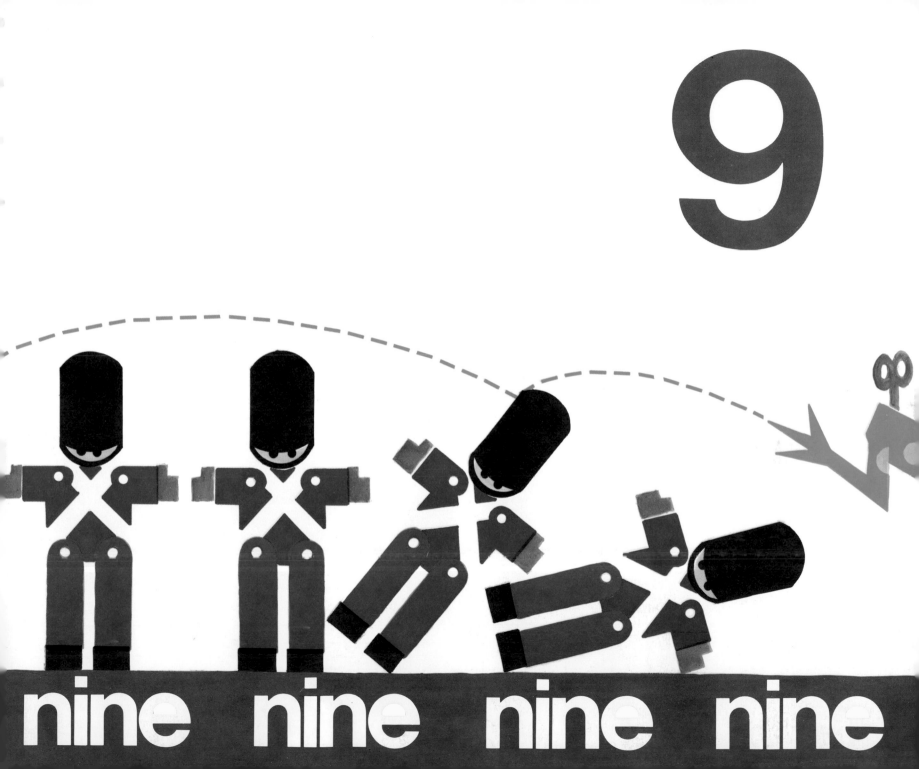

9

nine nine nine nine

ten ten ten ten ten

10

ten ten ten ten ten

But wait. He's stopped. He's on the ground. He's up. He's down. He's...all......unwound.